A Democracy Divided

Ralph J. Long Jr.

A Publication of The Poetry Box®

Editing & Book Design by Shawn Aveningo Sanders.
Cover Design by Robert R. Sanders.

ISBN: 978-1-948461-07-8
Printed in the United States of America.

Published by The Poetry Box®, 2018
Beaverton, Oregon
ThePoetryBox.com

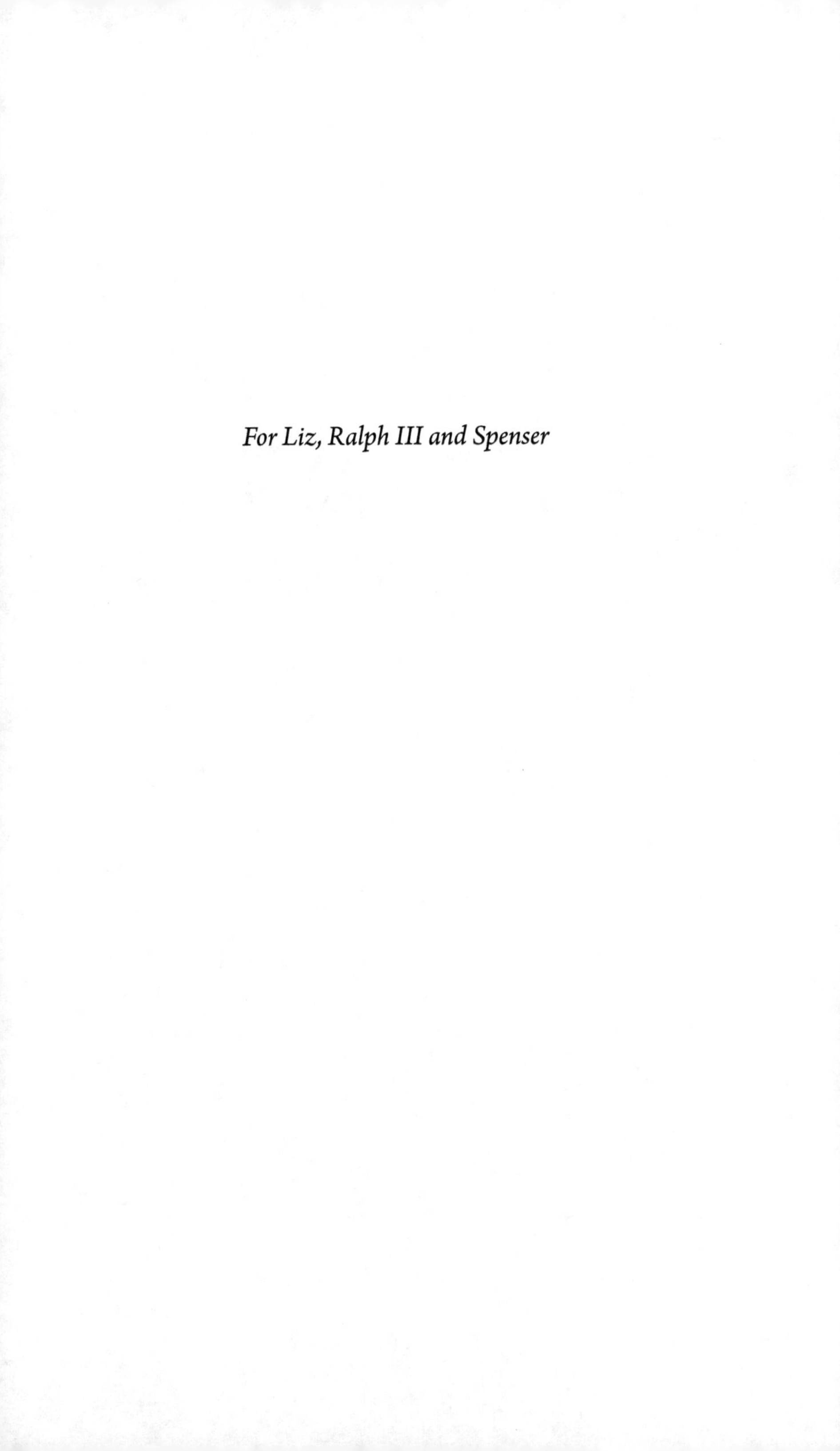

For Liz, Ralph III and Spenser

Contents

21st Century Reflections

on the

Bill of Rights

Amendment I

Congress shall make no law respecting an establishment of religion, or prohibiting the free exercise thereof; or abridging the freedom of speech, or of the press; or the right of the people peaceably to assemble, and to petition the Government for a redress of grievances.

Kaepernick's Knee

Under the aegis of hallowed freedom
Bedrock law protects inflaming words
Allowing Robertson's televised tirade
Promising Hurricane Sandy as God's plan
To stop Pagan Mormon Romney
Franklin Graham stands at the State House
Proclaiming Christianity is in the line of fire
While Westboro Baptist Church offers prayer
As screeds of homosexual hatred
Denying fallen soldiers families requiem honor
But when Kaepernick takes a silent knee
Derision and death threats become accepted
Free speech seems limited to those
Inclined to fundamental agreements

Amendment II

A well regulated Militia, being necessary to the security of a free State, the right of the people to keep and bear Arms, shall not be infringed.

In re: Baton Rouge Falcon Heights Dallas and Chicago

Civic worship intones universal justice
While acolytes of the second revision
To the ancient codification of frontier ideals
React with bombastic fervor as scrutiny
Confirms death is the truth of their zealotry
Ignoring chalked outlines on bloody sidewalks
And unending tears from racked broken mothers
Enured to accident, passion and malice
Unwilling to engage in discourse and
Convinced of inviolate armed rights above
Promised life, liberty and happiness
They parade with totemic weapons
Reveling in a delusion of self-protection
Hastening an unnecessary apocalypse

Amendment III

No Soldier shall, in time of peace be quartered in any house, without the consent of the Owner, nor in time of war, but in a manner to be prescribed by law.

Defenders

In this age of warring peace
The exorcism of George III complete
Cities and blue states no longer fear
Intruding soldiers of the nation
At desert camps and swampy bases
Underpaid warriors are kept apart
Their deadly battles are gamers' turns
For those who never followed commands
Come Memorial and Veterans Days
Politicians pay spare lip service
Vacuous platitudes do not honor
Unwanted unwell unhoused unfed
Veterans holding signs at off ramps
Isn't this a greater threat to liberty

Amendment IV

The right of the people to be secure in their persons, houses, papers, and effects, against unreasonable searches and seizures, shall not be violated, and no Warrants shall issue, but upon probable cause, supported by Oath or affirmation, and particularly describing the place to be searched, and the persons or things to be seized.

The Founding Fathers Consider Electronic Surveillance

Viewed through a terror shattered lens
All words: research, personal expression
And youthful stupidity may be criminal
When selected for prosecutorial review
Or self-promoting Congressional hearings
For us, a man's letters damned him if not burned
His spoken words held hostage to witnesses
Not an endless library of captured communications
All criminal cases were to be well founded
Apolitical when possible given human failings
Limited warrants sworn by men of conscience
Not *in camera* outlines of conspiratorial fears
Carried out by persons cajoled or coerced
In a fervor of frightened patriotism

Amendment V

No person shall be held to answer for a capital, or otherwise infamous crime, unless on a presentment or indictment of a Grand Jury, except in cases arising in the land or naval forces, or in the Militia, when in actual service in time of War or public danger; nor shall any person be subject for the same offence to be twice put in jeopardy of life or limb; nor shall be compelled in any criminal case to be a witness against himself, nor be deprived of life, liberty, or property, without due process of law; nor shall private property be taken for public use, without just compensation.

Double Jeopardy

> The media called for harsh action
> Despite the conflicted evidence
> Citizens enraged at the jury's verdict
> Defendants freed but shattered
> Incarceration almost a lesser deprivation
> Than life savaged by prosecutor's words
> Paraded in court as full due process
> In reality an audition for higher office
> Unsatisfied editorialists rant for justice
> Firing mob anger in city streets
> In the rush to quell passions
> Jurisdictional legerdemain presents
> A federal chance for conviction
> The accused to the dock again

Amendment VI

In all criminal prosecutions, the accused shall enjoy the right to a speedy and public trial, by an impartial jury of the State and district wherein the crime shall have been committed, which district shall have been previously ascertained by law, and to be informed of the nature and cause of the accusation; to be confronted with the witnesses against him; to have compulsory process for obtaining witnesses in his favor, and to have the Assistance of Counsel for his defence.

Plea or Trial?

He rolled the dice and rejected a plea
To risk a greater penalty against acquittal
Gambling on the overworked D.A.'s staff
And citizens who lives are unlike his
The strung out unbailed junkie arrives
On the sheriff's bus each morning
He seeks an impartial focused jury
Instead jurors having failed to be excused
Sit annoyed at the sequestering of cellphones
Stewing in brittle boredom unwilling
To contemplate the defendant's view of events
More concerned about bosses and day care
Their collective wish to have the trial over
Speed not justice guides their deliberations

Amendment VII

In Suits at common law, where the value in controversy shall exceed twenty dollars, the right of trial by jury shall be preserved, and no fact tried by a jury, shall be otherwise re-examined in any Court of the United States, than according to the rules of the common law.

Contingency Fee Nation

Civil trial options are a boon for
Opportunists with aggressive attorneys
Seeking rewards for acts of dubious intelligence
Tortious claims for driving with hot coffee
Open in one's lap or blaming a landlord
For a bathroom fall during intercourse
Become gleeful fodder for media outlets
If jurors decide to enrich the claimants
Subtler lawyers achieve financial success
Taking advantage of corporate anxieties
They fund Class Action suits never intended for trial
Offering settlement terms with non-disclosure agreements
To settle unproven claims of liabilities without ever
Facing a courtroom's truth-valuing crucible

Amendment VIII

Excessive bail shall not be required, nor excessive fines imposed, nor cruel and unusual punishments inflicted.

The Bondsman's Ten Percent

Speeding in a borrowed car, lights flashed in the mirror
He talked back to a tired cop who said to pop the trunk
Legal Aid cannot do much about the gun today
It is time to pay or share a cell as Arpaio's guest
The jail house gate has a heavy toll
For freedom until the appointed court date
Magistrate sets bond at one hundred thousand
Stocking job pays nine dollars an hour
No savings, wages garnished, child support overdue
With a credit score so low no one will lend
His grandmother's house as surety
To have the bail bond be delivered
All is ready except for the fee he cannot pay
Ten percent owed even if the charges are dismissed

Amendment IX

The enumeration in the Constitution, of certain rights, shall not be construed to deny or disparage others retained by the people.

Other Rights Retained by the People

Daring framers: bolder than today's interpreters
Joined together to throw off a king
Revolting to ensure their rights and liberty
Even as they counted blacks as three fifths a man
Backwards looks do not build the future
Societies twist and turn, change and evolve
Content with *stare decis* as the safe guide
Reluctant tribunals ignore the rising tides
In extremis war and protest force justice upon
Those lacking the bravery of the first honored rebels
Who knew founding documents were
Hope expressed not immutable holy writ
Original intent acknowledged unstated rights
Lighting the path for *Brown, Loving, and Obergefell*

Amendment X

The powers not delegated to the United States by the Constitution, nor prohibited by it to the States, are reserved to the States respectively, or to the people.

The Great Unknowns

What is reserved? What is prohibited?
Undefined and unallocated powers
What is the state? Who are the people?
Imagined and unimagined powers
Where should authority rest?
Within this Pandora's Box of questions
Calls to the dissatisfied resound
With partisan absolutism rampant
Its uncompromising devastation echoes
The intransigence that lead to civil war
As our gridlocked government fumes over
Abortion, healthcare and marriage
Rhetorical passions morph to threaten lives
Is this freedom: gift or devastation's harbinger?

Electoral ABC

The form of these lines was inspired by Robert Pinsky's marvelous 1999 consideration of the end of life, "ABC."

Their substance arises from the antagonistic political climate.

ABC—Cleveland

Atavistic brazen candidate
Declaims economics' fearful grip

Howling intolerant jeremiads
Knowing lies matter not

Ordinary politicians quietly recede
Seeing terror's unsavory visage waxing:

Xenophobic yawing zealotry

BCD—Arizona

Borders crush dreams
Erasing faith:
Greed's hand impoverishes

Journeyers keen
Latina Mothers never
Overcome parting's quiet

Razor sharp tears unanswered
Victims wander xeriscapes
Youth zigzags away

CDE—New York

Covers defend editors' favorites
Gotham heeds incendiary journalists

Kardashian lives magic
News or Post
Quality rarely sustained

Truth unneeded
Variety wins
Xmas Yard Zombies are best

DEF—Port Eads

Devastating epochal floods
Growing heat inversions
Joyless kin lament
Marsh nature obliterated

Polluted quicksilver river
Surging torrents uncontrolled

Vibrating wondering xylophone

Young zoological activists
Belittled Cassandras

EFG—Alabama

Eternally fierce god harshly invoked
Jettisoned kindness lessened morality

No-Nothing observers persuasive
Questioners rattle sager teachers
Unifying visions wane

Xeroxed yearning Zionists
Abandon biblical commands daily

Do Not Forget—Origins

Armenia Belize Cambodia

Denmark England France

Germany Haiti India

Japan Kenya Latvia

Mexico Nigeria Oman

Poland Qatar Russia

Senegal Turkey Ukraine

Vanuatu Wales X-(Stateless)

Yemen Zaire

FGH—Oklahoma

Firearms glorify hysteria
Imaginative jurisprudence

Killers leach machismo
Neglect others pain

Quaint reassurances slaughter trust
Undermining voter's worlds

Xanax yoked zestfulness
Avers bombastic creeds
Death endures

GHI—Vermont

Generation's hopes ignite
Justice's kindling lights
Millennial's new opinions

Positive questioning resounds
Socialist transmutes urgent voices
Willful X-Generation yells

Zillion affirmations blaring
Championing democracy
Endorsing freedom

HIJ—Topeka

Heavenly ideas juxtaposed
Kansas lowers margins needlessly
Outcast poor quake

Reactionaries severing taxes
Undoing values
Wounding Xenia, Yocemento, Zimmerdale

Acting because conservatives desire
Education featuring Godhead

IJK—Wyoming

Iraq journey knowingly lengthened
Misguided neocons overpromised
Putrid quicksand region
Saps troops unending valor

Wishful xyst yackers
Zeno's arrow baffling
Congress demands endless feats
Guaranteeing harm

JKL—New Jersey

Jabs kept landing
Marring national obsessions
Prospects quickly rebounded

Sycophantic tributes undertaken
Viciously whirling xylol
Yammering zero acceptance

Bitter conscience
Dreaming elevated future
Governor's hagiography implodes

Do Not Forget—Faiths

Animist Baptist Catholic

Druid Episcopal Fundamentalist

Gnostic Hindu Islam

Jewish Kachina Lutheran

Mormon Naturalist Orthodox

Presbyterian Quaker Rastafarian

Shaker Taoist Unitarian

Voodoo Wiccan X-(Other)

Yazidi Zoroastrian

KLM—Kentucky

Kindred leaders malign
Newfound opposition
Pretending queries restrict
Senators trod undeterred

Vacuous worldviews
Xenolithic yarns zing
Across broadcast channels

Deceived electorate freely gamed
Honored in jest

LMN—Coastal Florida

Lying media narcissist
Oversells Putin's quickness
Rejecting sager tacks

Unfazed voracious wannabe
X-radiates yesterday's Zeitgeist
Assertions boasted callously

Dealmaker eager
For great homage
Inspires justifying knaves

MNO—District of Columbia

Merrick noting objections perseveres
Quixotic resolved supreme

Trial unconvened vote waylaid
X-rated yielders zoom away
Bi-partisan congeniality

Denying evaluation
Forgoing governance hurdles
Ideology jawbones knotted law

NOP—Pennsylvania

News' oblique predictions
Quote radicalized suburbanites
Triumph unbound

Voters watch xenophobia yawping
Zen abuts Babel

Confounded demographic elites
Frightened
Grasping
Hear independence jeopardized

Keystoners lack momentum

OPQ—Indiana

Obama presidency quests restricted
Savage tirades undercut valiant work

X-Boxers yerk Zzzz's
Adults binge cable

Discouraged elders follow
Grandiose Hannity incantations
Journalistic kabbalism
Lucidity's maximum nadir

Do Not Forget—Battles

Alamo Bunker Hill Coral Sea

Detroit Erie Fredericksburg

Guadalcanal Hue Iwo Jima

Java Sea Korea Leyte

Manassas New Orleans Omaha Beach

Pearl Harbor Quebec Remagen

Saigon Ticonderoga Unsan

Vicksburg Wilderness X-(Hidden)

Ypres Z-(Yet to Come)

PQR—Texas

Pulsing quorums reverberating
Statisticians trembling
Unverifiable visionaries writhing

Xenial yes-men zippers askew
Blather conflicted demonic expiations

Feminist gains hazard immature justifiers
Knowledge leaves morose nabobs obliterated

QRS—Mississippi

Quislings resolutely self-interested
Television underscoring vanity
Wordy, xeric, yo-yoing
Zenless assertive blamers

Catharsis demeans evidence
Faulty gerrymanders help
Inflame jingoists

Klan lurks menacingly
Nationalism obscures perils

RST—Chicago

Racism's sere tinder
Underpins violent wastelands
X-town's youth zapped

Assault bullets careen
Desperation envelops families
Gangrenous hearts incite juvenile killers

Liberal moralists nod
Overseeing police quagmires

STU—Raleigh

Sexist Trumplandia unravels
Victim's witnessing
XX-chromosomes yell:
Zoos are better climates

Defiance erodes fascist gravity
Harasser's insults judicial kudzu

Lustful misogynist nears oblivion
P-word quashes republican

TUV—California

Traumatized urban vigilantes
Witnessing xanthous Y-linked zeal
Accost barbaric crusaders destroy efforts
Favoring greater humanity

Imperative justice keeps losing
Making noxious overeager prosecutors
Quintessential Republican stars

Do Not Forget—Leaders

Adams Brandeis Chavez

Du Bois Evers Ford

Glenn Holmes Inouye

Jefferson King Lincoln

Milk Nader Obama

Parks Quill Roosevelt

Sanger Tubman Udall

Vernon Washington Malcom X

Young Zenger

UVW—Idaho

Universal video wistfully x-raying
Yenning zaniest actors

Blistered country delirious
Electoral factions grappling:
Hold inchoate jamborees

Kicking liberty mercilessly
New origins prohibited
Quarrelling raw scenes televised

VWX—Montana

Valuing walls:
Xenic Yankee zones
Accept being cowed

Disinformation equals freedom
Grotesque hateful innuendo joined

Katabolic lurching minions nurture
Obsequious pliant queues
Repeating splintering tirades
Unquestioned

WXY—Georgia

Wandering xebecs
Yardarms zipped:
Arrive bearing colonists
Displacing embedded free groups

Historic identifications jolted
Known lands menaced
Natives organize
Primitive quivering response

Steadfast tides unload victors

XYZ—Nevada

Xanadu yields zilch
Accelerating blunders crush

Desperate ego flailing
Generating hateful id jokes
Keeping lipid mogul noticed

Overnight precious Q-score raveling
Sad titan unleashes vitriolic warnings

YZA—Alaska

Yahooing Zeligs abet broad calumny
Democratic enthusiasms flayed grossly

Hammering internet judgements
Kayo legitimate mediations

Nonsensical orations polarize
Quarrelsome rooters savor turmoil
Urging vindictive withering xenogenesis

Do Not Forget—Future Generations

Ava Benjamin Carlos

Deirdre Eric Frances

Gwen Hannah Isaac

Jesus Karen Lamar

Mohamed Nancy Oscar

Penny Quincy Rishi

Sarah Tonya Ursala

Vivienne Walker Xenia

Yvonne Zachary

ZAB—South Carolina

Zenith

Attacking Benghazi critics
Disregard established facts

Glib husband's infidelity
Jeering kvetchers lampoon marriage
Noble or politic quotient

Repelling sexist taunts
Undaunted vision

Women's xeric year

Notes

The work depends on words that are not normally used in conversation, especially words beginning with K, X, Y & Z. The following definitions may be of interest.

Katabolic: having a destructive metabolism.

Kabbalistic: possessing a hidden meaning.

Keystoner: a resident of Pennsylvania.

Xabob: an urban slang term for a childish or over emotional person.

Xanax: a widely prescribed drug for anxiety and panic disorders.

Xanthous: a race with yellowish hair.

Xebec: a three masted Mediterranean ship.

Xenial: friendliness between host and guest.

Xenic: a weak acid and oxidizer.

Xenogenesis: the production of offspring different from its parents.

Xenolithic: a rock fragment different from the igneous mass that contains it.

Xeric: a very dry habitat.

Xylol: a water insoluble, flammable, toxic chemical.

Xyst: a portico.

[…]

Yawping: to shout or exclaim hoarsely.

Yenning: longing or yearning.

Yerk: from the Scottish: to lash out.

Zeno's Arrow: one of the paradox's recounted by Aristotle.

Zelig: a person able to change appearance, behavior and attitudes, so as to be comfortable in any situation.

Port Eads is located at the mouth of the Mississippi River. It was destroyed by Hurricane Katrina. Xenia, Yocemento and Zimmerdale are communities in Kansas.

About the Author

Ralph J. Long Jr. is a retired investment executive whose career featured extensive travel throughout the United States. He was born in Brooklyn, New York and has lived in Northern California for thirty three years. He received a Bachelor of Arts in Political Science from Haverford College and did graduate business studies at New York University.

His poetry has appeared in *Stoneboat Literary Journal*, *The Poeming Pigeon*, *The Ghazal Page* and *The Avocet*. He resides in Oakland, California with his wife, Liz and their sons. He is currently at work on a series of epistolary poems addressed to poets and writers that reflect on modern America, travel and his youth.

About The Poetry Box®

The Poetry Box® was founded by Shawn Aveningo Sanders & Robert R. Sanders, who wholeheartedly believe that every day spent with the people you love, doing what you love, is a moment in life worth cherishing. Their boutique press celebrates the talents of their fellow artisans and writers through professional book design and publishing of individual collections, as well as their flagship literary journal, *The Poeming Pigeon.*

Feel free to visit the online bookstore (thePoetryBox.com), where you'll find more titles including:

Keeping It Weird: Poems & Stories of Portland, Oregon

The Way a Woman Knows by Carolyn Martin

Giving Ground by Lynn M. Knapp

Broadfork Farm by Tricia Knoll

Impressions by Dr. Paul T.M. Jackson

Psyche's Scroll by Karla Linn Merrifield

Painting the Heart Open by Liz Nakazawa

An Eyeful of Hennepin Neon by Rheanna Haaland

Fireweed by Gudrun Bortman

My Life in Cars by Linda Strever

and more . . .

"At a time in our history when it's easy to feel overwhelmed and hopeless, Ralph J. Long Jr. asks us to consider the strange yet beautiful language of our American Bill of Rights, the possibilities of formal poetry, and complicated issues of social justice and history. With a sharp eye, big-hearted intelligence, and a certain buoyant energy, the poet looks closely at our shared American situation, our 'fervor of frightened patriotism.' *A Democracy Divided* is a pertinent, powerful and original collection indeed."

~ Caroline Goodwin, author of *Peregrine*
and *Paper Tree*

"Ralph J. Long Jr. links a nation's founding to its current crisis in an unflinching snapshot of our sociopolitical climate, and an indictment of the sensationalist figureheads who fan the flames of our slow undoing."

~ Josh Gaines, Thoughtcrime Press, editor
Not My President: The Anthology of Dissent

US $ 12.00